James, thank you for all your love and support.
You are my greatest wish come true.
—Melissa

To all dreamers who believe in the power of wishes.
—Khoa

Text Copyright © 2023 Melissa Stiveson
Illustration Copyright © 2023 Khoa Le
Design Copyright © 2023 Sleeping Bear Press

SLEEPING BEAR PRESS™
2395 South Huron Parkway, Suite 200, Ann Arbor, MI 48104
www.sleepingbearpress.com © Sleeping Bear Press

Printed and bound in the United States
10 9 8 7 6 5 4 3 2 1

ISBN: 978-1-53411-175-2

Library of Congress Cataloging-in-Publication on file.
Photo credits: Kite festival: Lucy.Brown / Shutterstock.com
Birthday cake: PeopleImages.com - Yuri A / Shutterstock.com
Wishing star: Yuganov Konstantin / Shutterstock.com
Wishing tree: dotshock / Shutterstock.com
Loi Krathong: Elizaveta Galitckaia / Shutterstock.com
Dandelion: sindlera / Shutterstock.com
Trevi Fountain: TTstudio / Shutterstock.com
Butterfly: ballycroy / iStockphoto.com
Four leaf clover: Leigh Prather / Shutterstock.com

WISHES
of the World

By Melissa Stiveson

Illustrated by Khoa Le

PUBLISHED *by* SLEEPING BEAR PRESS™

A wondrous possibility takes shape
And hums in my heart.

It thrums and strums into a wild wish.

Hope swirls and whirls
As I search for the words

To make my wish just right.
My wish wants to be free.

And I want to give it the best chance of coming true,
So I ask, how do you send your wish into the world?

In Guatemala . . .

I pen my wish on parchment and tie it to the tail of a giant kite,

Which bobs and weaves in a kaleidoscope of color,

And soars with my wish, higher and higher.

In the United States . . .

At twilight's first twinkle,

I wish on a shining star,

To fulfill my wish while I dream.

In South Africa . . .

I blow out bright birthday candles.

The flames flicker and fade into wisps of smoke,

Wafting my wish off to faraway places.

In Japan . . .
I carefully craft a note,
String it with bright ribbon and hang it from bamboo,
Where my wish dances with the wind.

In Thailand . . .

I set a lighted candle inside a paper boat,

Murmur my wish by moonlight,

And set my wish free upon the winding river.

In France . . .

I close my eyes and whoosh my wish.

Dandelion puffs spin and drift away,

To sprout my wish in rich, soft soil.

In Italy . . .

I think my wish upon a shiny coin,

And toss it over my shoulder into a fountain,

Where my wish shimmers and glimmers in the sparkling water.

In Native American Cultures . . .

I whisper my wish upon the wings of a butterfly
Perched on my palm,
Then watch the butterfly flit and flutter my wish beyond the horizon.

In Ireland . . .

If I am lucky enough to find a four-leaf clover, I tell it my wish

And pluck it and tuck it in a secret spot,

As my wish waits for the perfect moment to come true.

There are so many wondrous ways to wish.

My wish for you—

Wherever you wish, however you wish—

is for all *your* wishes to come true.

THE TRADITION *of* MAKING A WISH
IS A UNIVERSAL EXPERIENCE,
AND THERE ARE MANY TRADITIONS *to* RELEASE
WISHES INTO *the* WORLD.

On November 1st, during the All Saints' Day festival in Guatemala, giant kites of all colors create a kaleidoscope in the sky. Families write wishes on paper, tie them to the kite tails, and send the wishes heavenward, where they believe deceased ancestors intercept them. The ancestors do what they can to help ensure the wish comes true. This tradition, which is held in the local cemetery, has been practiced for over three thousand years.

American children wish on the first star they see in the night sky and whisper this nursery rhyme:

"Star light, star bright,
The first star I see tonight.
I wish I may, I wish I might,
Have the wish I wish tonight."

For the wish to come true, the child must keep it secret.

Ancient Greeks topped round cakes with candles to mimic the shape of the moon and the moon's glow. In Germany, this practice was adapted to add candles to birthday cakes — one candle for each year plus one more for "a year to grow on." With eyes closed, the birthday kid makes a silent wish while blowing out the candles. For the wish to come true, the wish must be kept secret and all the candles blown out in one breath. In some ways, this tradition has been adopted all over the globe.

Visitors to some Japanese temples write a wish on paper and hang it on bamboo in the courtyard. Bamboo grows tall and straight, taking the wish as high as it can. The tradition of wishing trees is found in many countries, including Scotland, Denmark, England, and Belgium.

The New Year's festival of Loi Krathong is celebrated in Thailand during a full moon. Children and adults set a small lighted candle or dessert in a boat made of leaves or paper. The wish is spoken, and the boat is set on the river. The boat carries the wish downriver and removes negative past experiences, allowing room for the wish to be fulfilled.

Traditionally in France, young girls blew on dandelion puffs to determine if their love interest returned their feelings. Now, dandelions are used to make wishes of all kinds. The wisher focuses on the wish with eyes closed, and then blows the seeds far and wide. If all the seeds are blown from the stem, the wish will come true. If any seeds are left, they grab another dandelion and wish again.

In Rome, children and adults toss coins into the famous Trevi Fountain. The tradition is to toss the coin over a shoulder into the fountain, eyes closed. It is believed the wish will come true if the coin lands in the fountain's water. All over the globe, people wish and toss coins into fountains.

Native American cultures describe a child capturing a butterfly, telling it a wish, and setting it free. The butterfly will keep the wish a secret and divulge it only to the Creator. The child must release the butterfly for the wish to come true.

For centuries, the Irish have considered four-leaf clovers lucky. Chances of finding a stem with the fourth leaf are one in ten thousand. The leaves stand for hope, faith, love, and luck. Those lucky enough to find a four-leaf clover make a silent wish over the clover and keep it out of sight. If someone else glimpses the clover, the wish will not come true.

THERE ARE MANY WAYS *to* WISH.
FIND A WAY THAT FEELS RIGHT TO YOU
AND SET YOUR WISH FREE!